JAZZ PIANO SOLOS   VOLUME 37

silver screen jazz

Arranged by Brent Edstrom

contents

ISBN 978-1-4950-1731-5

HAL•LEONARD®
CORPORATION

7777 W. BLUEMOUND RD. P.O. BOX 13819 MILWAUKEE, WI 53213

Visit Hal Leonard Online at
www.halleonard.com

ALFIE
Theme from the Paramount Picture ALFIE

Words by HAL DAVID
Music by BURT BACHARACH

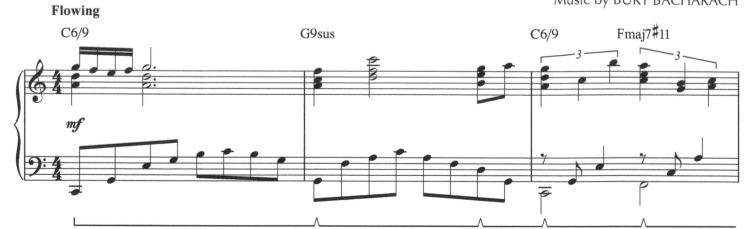

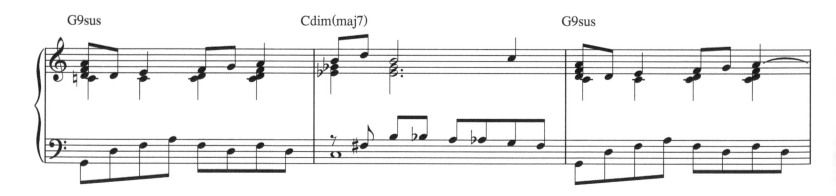

AS TIME GOES BY

from CASABLANCA

Words and Music by
HERMAN HUPFELD

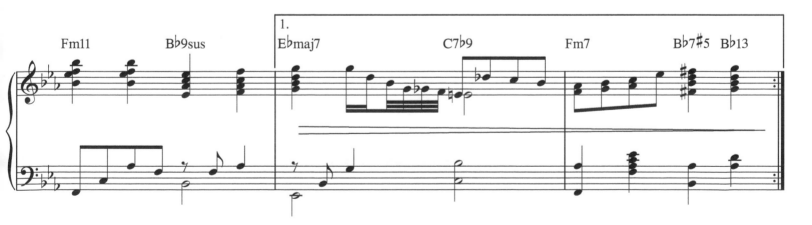

BÉSAME MUCHO
(Kiss Me Much)
featured in MONA LISA SMILE

Music and Spanish Words by
CONSUELO VELAZQUEZ
English Words by SUNNY SKYLAR

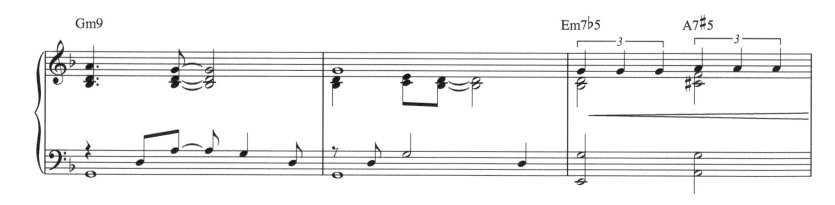

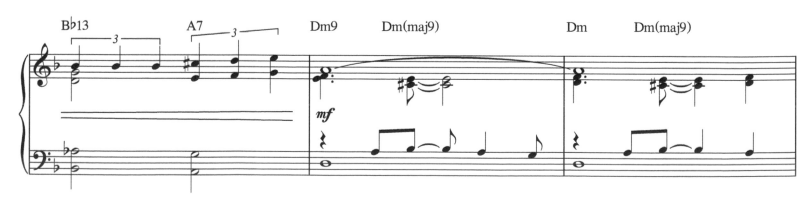

COME RAIN OR SHINE

from ST. LOUIS WOMAN

Words by JOHNNY MERCER
Music by HAROLD ARLEN

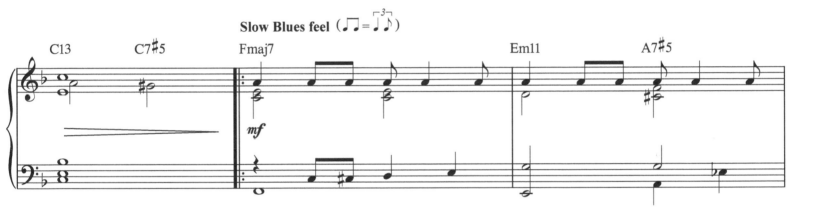

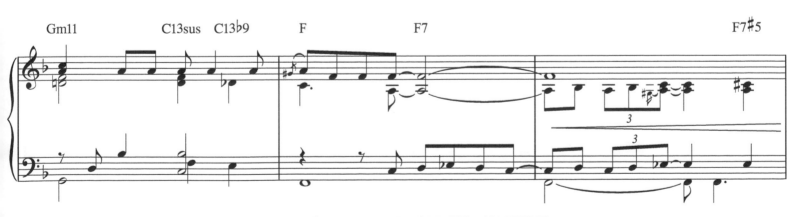

CALL ME IRRESPONSIBLE

from the Paramount Picture PAPA'S DELICATE CONDITION

Words by SAMMY CAHN
Music by JAMES VAN HEUSEN

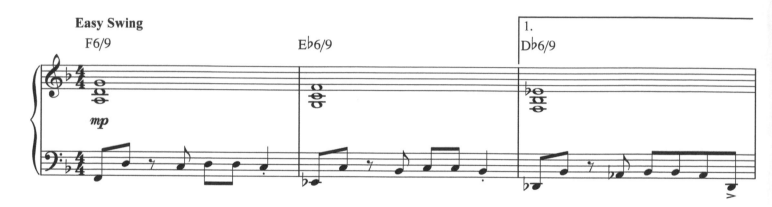

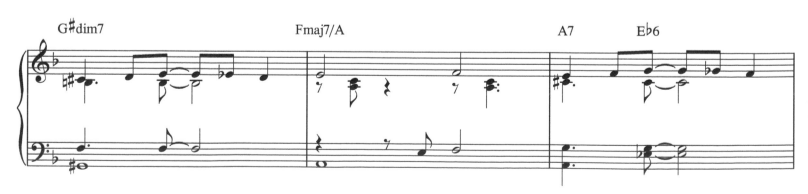

THE CONTINENTAL
from THE GAY DIVORCEE

Words by HERB MAGIDSON
Music by CON CONRAD

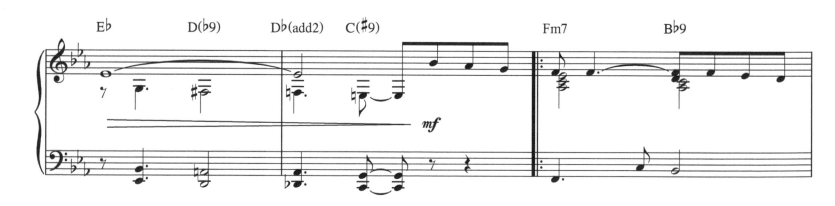

DAYS OF WINE AND ROSES

from DAYS OF WINE AND ROSES

Lyrics by JOHNNY MERCER
Music by HENRY MANCINI

Moderately fast Swing

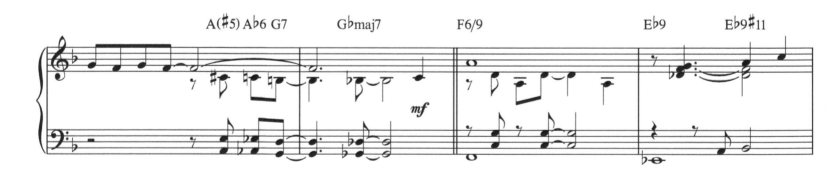

EASY LIVING
Theme from the Paramount Picture EASY LIVING

Words and Music by LEO ROBIN
and RALPH RAINGER

Moderately slow Swing

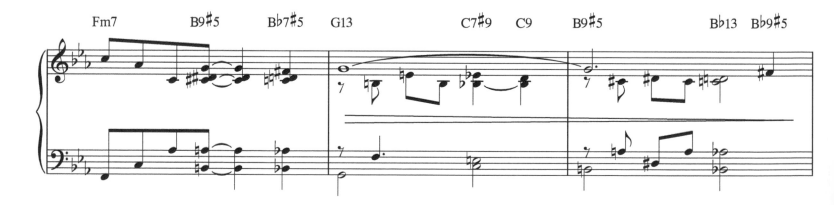

I HEAR A RHAPSODY
featured in CLASH BY NIGHT

By GEORGE FRAJOS,
JACK BAKER and DICK GASPARRE

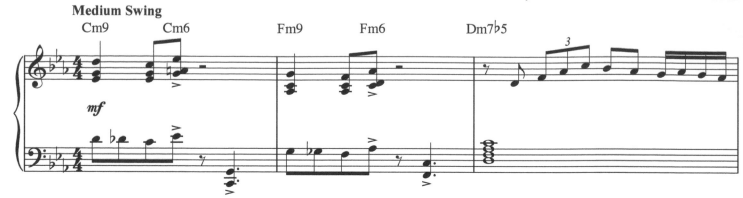

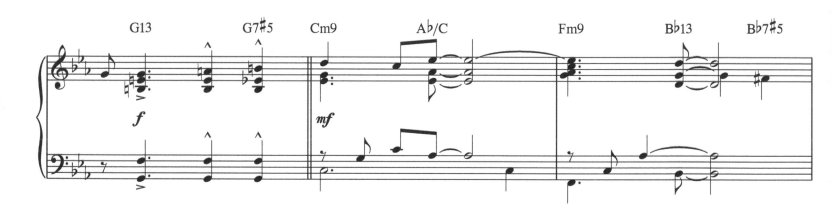

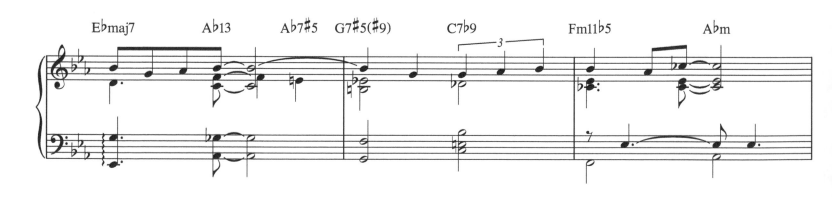

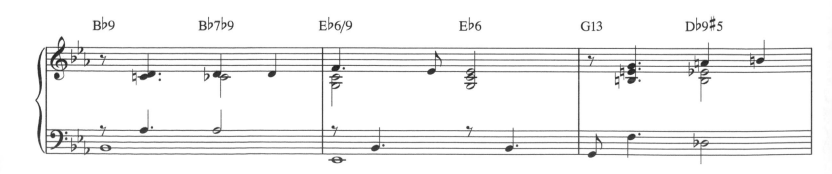

I REMEMBER YOU

from the Paramount Picture THE FLEET'S IN

Words by JOHNNY MERCER
Music by VICTOR SCHERTZINGER

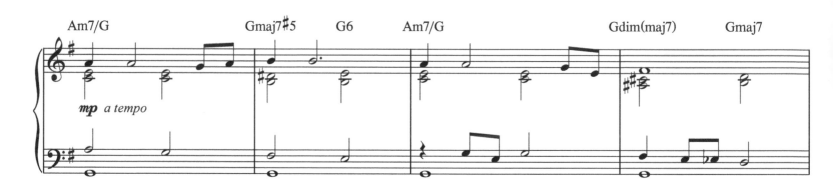

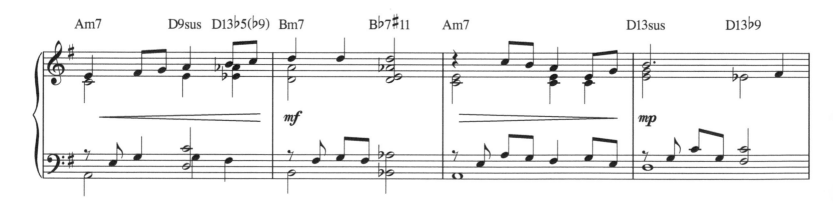

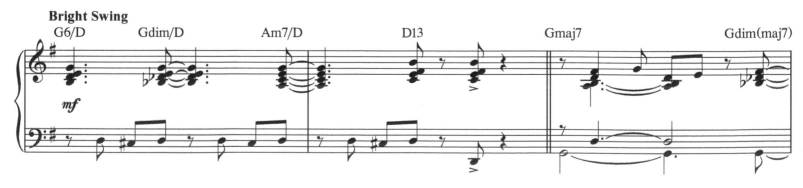

LAURA
from LAURA

Lyrics by JOHNNY MERCER
Music by DAVID RAKSIN

I'LL SEE YOU IN MY DREAMS

featured in KITTY FOYLE

Words by GUS KAHN
Music by ISHAM JONES

IT HAD TO BE YOU

featured in WHEN HARRY MET SALLY

Words by GUS KAHN
Music by ISHAM JONES

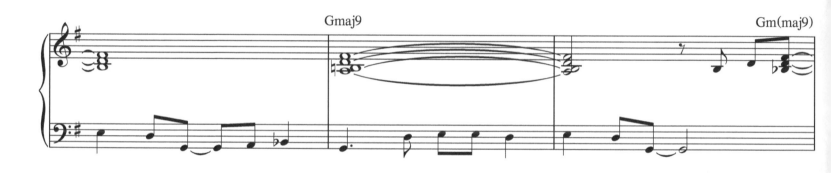

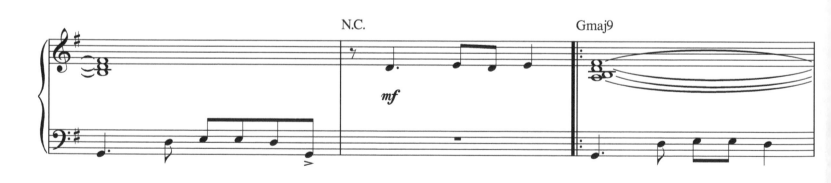

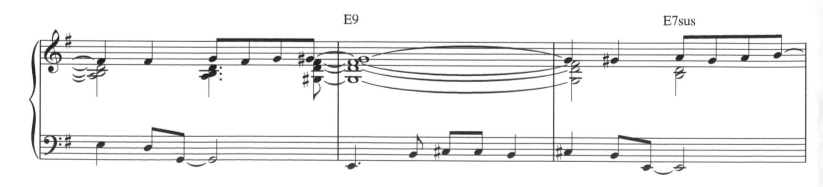

PORTRAIT OF JENNIE

from PORTRAIT OF JENNIE

Words by GORDON BURDGE
Music by J. RUSSEL ROBINSON

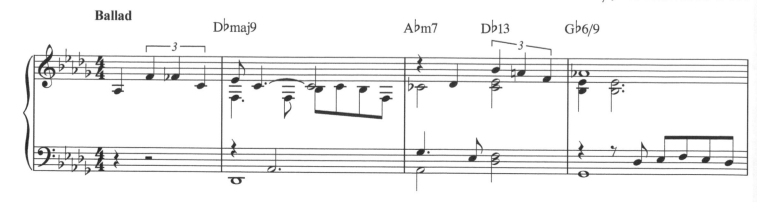

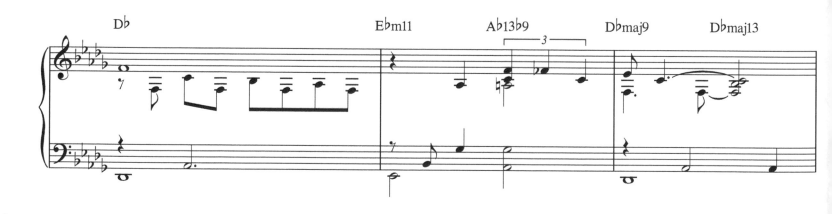

PURE IMAGINATION
from WILLY WONKA AND THE CHOCOLATE FACTORY

Words and Music by LESLIE BRICUSSE
and ANTHONY NEWLEY

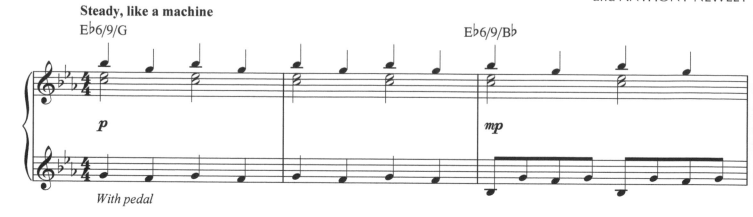

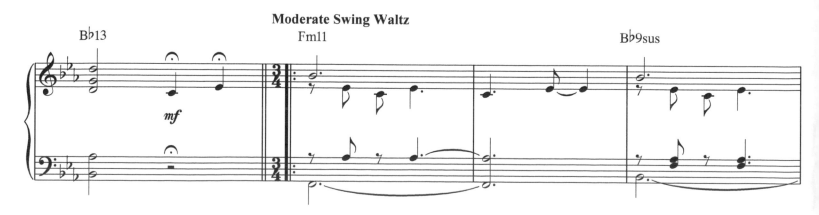

SECRET LOVE
from CALAMITY JANE

Words by PAUL FRANCIS WEBSTER
Music by SAMMY FAIN

Bright Swing

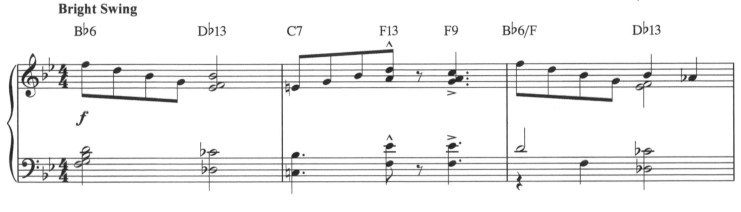

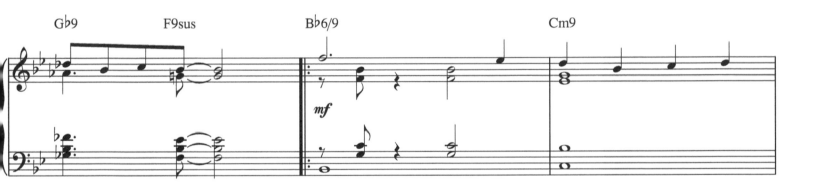

THE SHADOW OF YOUR SMILE
Love Theme from THE SANDPIPER

Music by JOHNNY MANDEL
Words by PAUL FRANCIS WEBSTER

Freely, with feeling

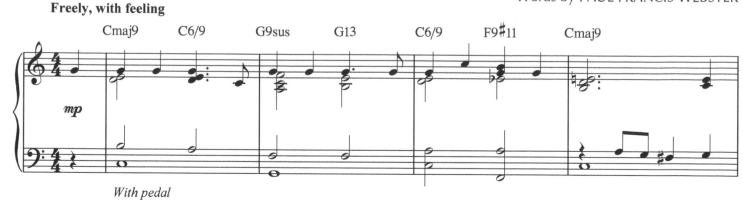

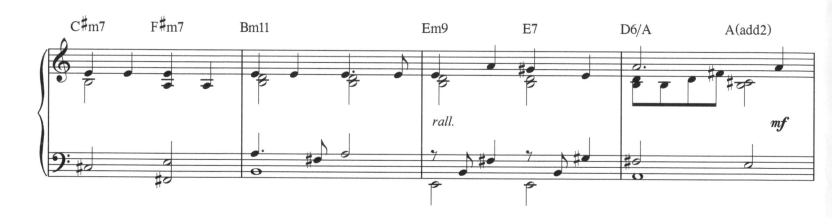

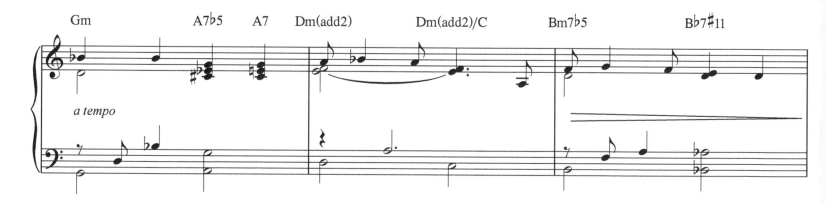

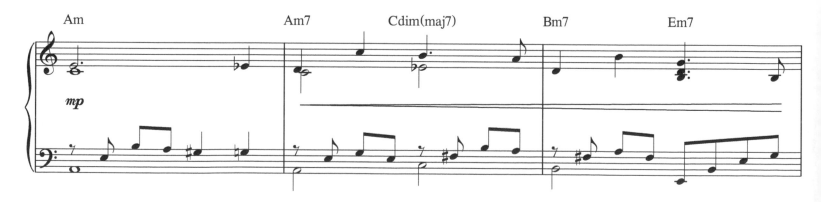

SMILE
from MODERN TIMES

Words by JOHN TURNER
and GEOFFREY PARSONS
Music by CHARLES CHAPLIN

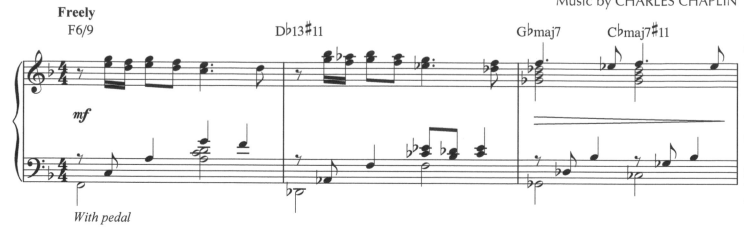

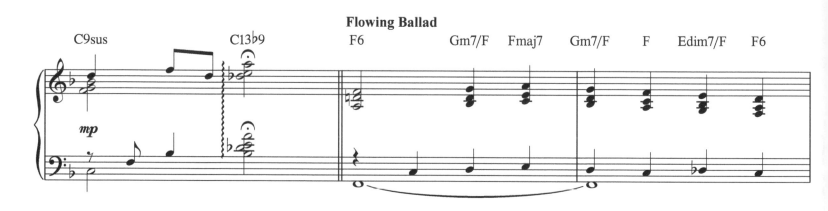

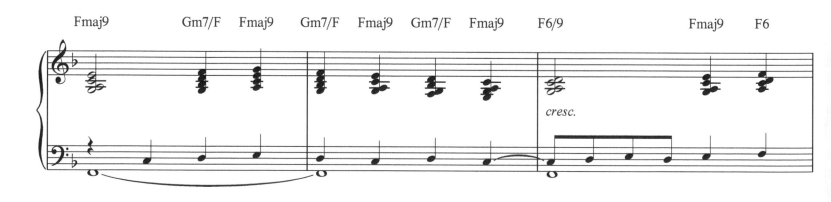

STELLA BY STARLIGHT
from the Paramount Picture THE UNINVITED

Words by NED WASHINGTON
Music by VICTOR YOUNG

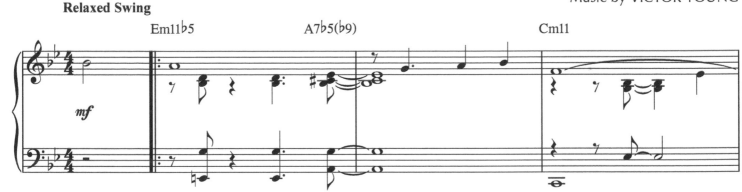

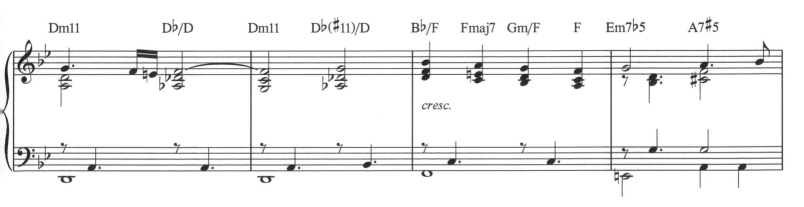

THIS TIME THE DREAM'S ON ME

from BLUES IN THE NIGHT

Words by JOHNNY MERCER
Music by HAROLD ARLEN

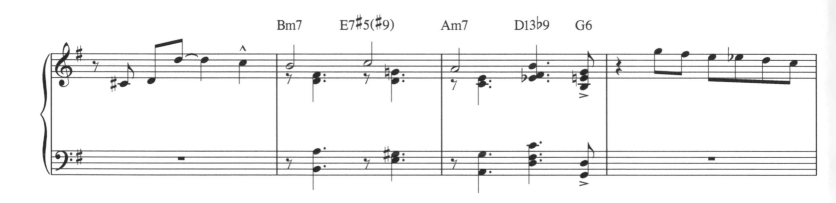

THREE COINS IN THE FOUNTAIN

from THREE COINS IN THE FOUNTAIN

Words by SAMMY CAHN
Music by JULE STYNE

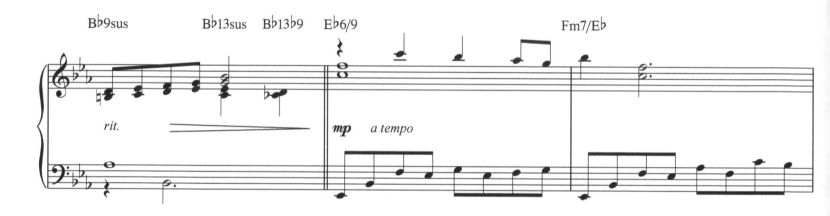

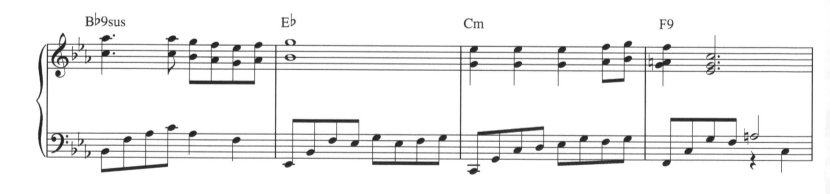

THE WAY YOU LOOK TONIGHT

from SWING TIME

Words by DOROTHY FIELDS
Music by JEROME KERN

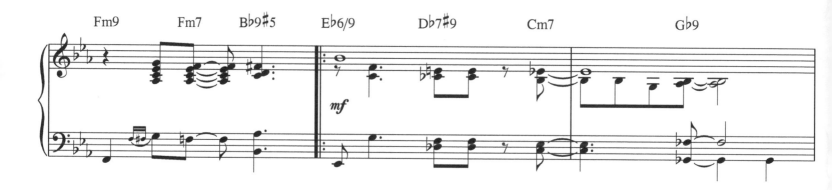

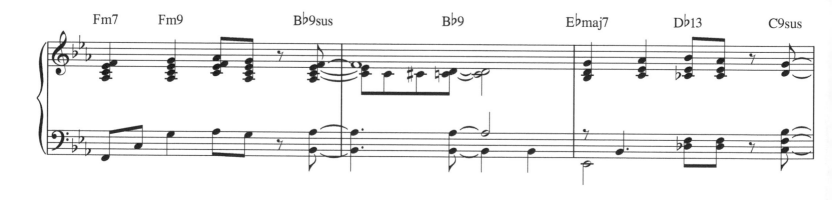

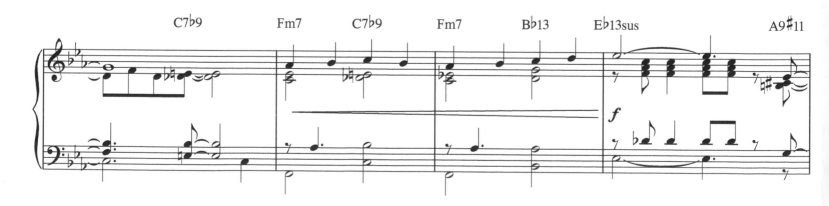

YOU'D BE SO NICE TO COME HOME TO

from SOMETHING TO SHOUT ABOUT

Words and Music by
COLE PORTER

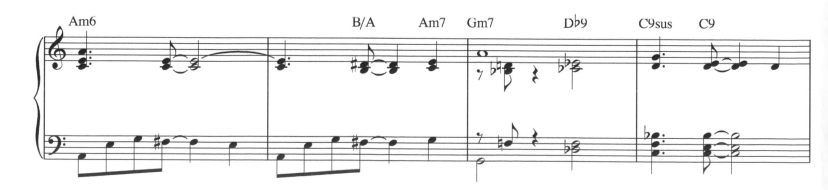

WHEN I GROW TOO OLD TO DREAM

featured in THE NIGHT IS YOUNG

Lyrics by OSCAR HAMMERSTEIN II
Music by SIGMUND ROMBERG

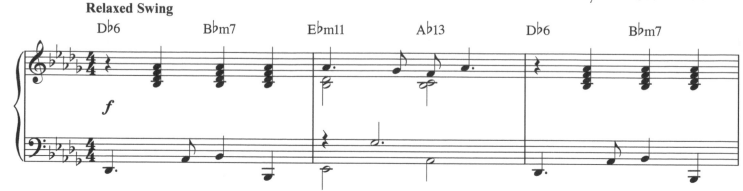

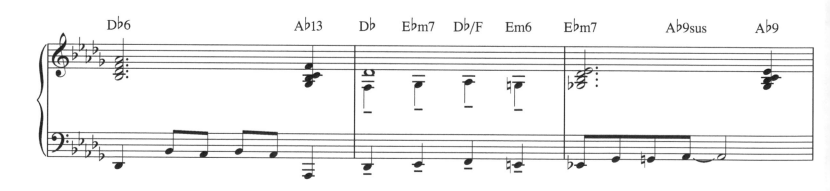